Hummingbirds

Victoria Blakemore

For Mom and Sir, with love to you in your cozy mountain

cabin. I miss you!

Copyright info/picture credits

Cover, Elizaveta kirina/Shutterstock; Page 3, Nicman/Pixabay; Page 5, weareone2017/Pixabay; Page 7, BarbeeAnne/Pixabay; Page 9, pattyjansen/Pixabay; Pages 10-11, CCat82/AdobeStock; Page 13, Richard/AdobeStock; Page 15, Dirgon/Pixabay; Page 17, ducken99/Pixabay; Page 19, skeeze/Pixabay; Page 21, ondrejprosicky/AdobeStock; Page 23; skeeze/Pixabay; Page 25, pixeldust/Pixabay; Page 27, mbolina/AdobeStock; Page 29, skeeze/Pixabay; Page 31, YanCabrera/Pixabay; Page 33, Elizaveta kirina/Shutterstock

Table of Contents

What are Hummingbirds?   2

Size   4

Physical Characteristics   6

Habitat   8

Range   10

Diet   12

Communication   16

Movement   18

Hummingbird Chicks   20

Hummingbird Life   22

Feeding Hummingbirds   24

Population   26

Hummingbirds in Danger   28

Helping Hummingbirds   30

Glossary   34

What Are Hummingbirds?

Hummingbirds are very small birds. They are related to swifts.

There are more than 300 kinds of hummingbirds. They differ in size, color, and where they are found. The bee hummingbird is the world's smallest bird.

Hummingbirds are known for their brightly colored feathers and long, thin beaks.

Size

Hummingbirds usually grow to be between two and five inches long. Some can grow to be up to eight inches long.

Since they are so small, hummingbirds do not weigh much. They weigh less than an ounce when they are fully grown.

Male hummingbirds are usually

a bit larger than female

hummingbirds.

Physical Characteristics

Hummingbirds have a long, thin beak. It is used to get nectar from flowers. Inside the beak is a long tongue.

Male hummingbirds have very brightly colored feathers. They shine in the sunlight and are used to **attract** a female.

Hummingbirds have short legs

and very small feet. They are

used to **perch** on branches.

Habitat

Hummingbirds are found in rainforests, forests, and meadows. Most prefer tropical **climates** where it is warm and areas with lots of plants.

Some hummingbirds **migrate** to warmer areas in the winter. They return to their home when the weather warms up again.

Range

Hummingbirds are found on every continent except Antarctica.

10

There are twelve different kinds
that are found in the United
States.

Diet

Hummingbirds are **omnivores**. They eat both meat and plants.

Their diet is made up of small insects, spiders, tree sap, pollen, and nectar from flowers.

Hummingbirds use their long tongues to lick their food. It moves very fast and can lick about thirteen times per second.

Hummingbirds have a very fast heartbeat and high body temperature. This means that they need to eat a lot of food and often.

When it gets cold, they go into a deep sleep called **torpor**. It allows them to use less energy and survive in the colder temperatures.

Hummingbirds help to **pollinate**

flowers. They spread pollen from

one flower to another when

they are eating.

Communication

Hummingbirds use sound and movement to communicate with each other. Although most hummingbirds do not sing, they can chirp and chatter.

They dart back and forth and move in different ways to send messages.

Different kinds of hummingbirds may use different sounds to communicate.

Movement

Hummingbirds do not have strong legs. They cannot walk. They are able to shuffle, but most of their movement is flying.

They get their name from the humming sound when they flap their wings. Their wings flap very fast, up to eighty times per second!

Hummingbirds can fly forward,

backward, and upside down!

They can hover in one place

by moving their wings in a

figure-eight pattern.

Hummingbird Chicks

Hummingbirds make a tiny nest out of plants and lichen. Then, they lay one or two eggs.

Mother hummingbirds sit on the eggs until they hatch into chicks. This usually takes about two weeks.

Mothers feed their babies until

they are old enough to feed

themselves.

Hummingbird Life

Hummingbirds are **solitary** animals. They spend most of their time alone.

They can be very **aggressive** when other hummingbirds get too close. They are likely to guard their food sources and chase other hummingbirds away.

Hummingbirds do not see very

well in the dark. They do most

of their flying during the day.

Feeding Hummingbirds

Some people plant flowers that hummingbirds like to **attract** them to their yard. Plants like trumpet flowers, bee balm, and honeysuckle are hummingbird favorites.

People also keep special hummingbird feeders in their yards.

A mixture of sugar and water

is poured into the feeder.

Hummingbirds like to drink it.

Population

Many different kinds of

hummingbirds are currently

endangered. There are not

many left in the wild.

Most hummingbirds are not

endangered, but many

different populations are

declining.

Hummingbirds are believed to

live between three or four years

in the wild.

Hummingbirds in Danger

The main threat that hummingbirds are facing is habitat loss. Their habitats are being destroyed for farmland, buildings, and roads.

Many hummingbirds are only found in one place. Any changes to their habitat can be a big problem for them.

Rising temperatures can also

affect how hummingbirds

migrate. It can make it harder

for them to find food.

Helping Hummingbirds

Many groups are working to help hummingbirds around the world. Some help hummingbirds that are sick or injured.

Others focus on research. They learn about hummingbirds so they can find other ways to help them.

Special **preserves** provide animals like hummingbirds with safe habitats to live in.

People can help hummingbirds right in their backyard. They can plant flowers that hummingbirds like or hang up feeders. This provides hummingbirds with more food sources.

Glossary

Aggressive: ready to fight, mean

Attract: to get the attention of, to cause to come near

Climate: the usual weather in a place

Declining: getting smaller

Endangered: at risk of becoming extinct

Migrate: to move from one place to another, usually because of colder temperatures or food availability

Nocturnal: animals that are active at night

Omnivore: an animal that eats both meat and plants

Perch: to sit or rest on a branch or bar

Pollinate: to move pollen from one plant to another

Preserve: a protected area of land that provides a safe habitat for plants and animals

Solitary: living alone

Torpor: a state of deep sleep when an animal's body temperature is lower and their heart rate slows down to use less energy, similar to hibernating

About the Author

Victoria Blakemore is a first grade

teacher in Southwest Florida with a

passion for reading.

You can visit her at

www.elementaryexplorers.com

Also in This Series

Gray Wolves	Sloths	Flamingos	Camels	Koalas	Honey Bees	Pandas
Pangolins	White-Tailed Deer	Orcas	Giraffes	Corn	Meerkats	Echidnas
Walruses	Raccoons	Bald Eagles	Apples	Arctic Foxes	Red Pandas	Cassowaries
Tigers	Ladybugs	Moose	Beluga Whales	Leopards	Elephants	Jellyfish
Binturongs	Lions	Dolphins	Reindeer	Hammerhead Sharks	Hippos	Pumpkins
Peafowl	Chameleons	Florida Panthers	Aye-Ayes	Black Bears	Cheetahs	Manatees
Gingerbread	Polar Bears	Hot Chocolate	Orangutans	Coyotes	Marshmallows	Strawberries

Victoria Blakemore

Also in This Series

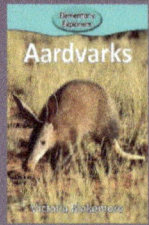

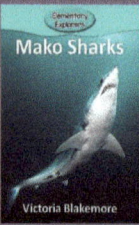

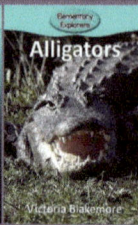

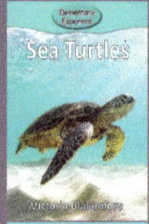

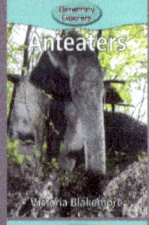

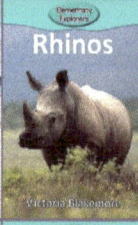

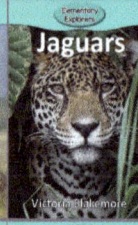

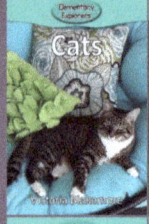

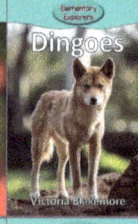

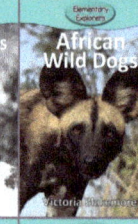

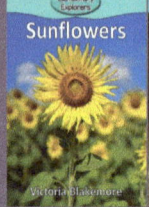

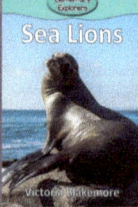

Aardvarks	Mako Sharks	Alligators	Frogs	Hedgehogs	Brown Bears	Bongos
Sea Turtles	Quokkas	Muskrats	Zebras	Red Foxes	Ring-Tailed Lemurs	Platypuses
Anteaters	Kangaroos	Rhinos	Jaguars	Wombats	Capybaras	Gorillas
Cats	Skunks	Butterflies	Dingoes	Snow Leopards	African Wild Dogs	Penguins
Whale Sharks	Wolverines	Warthogs	Caracals	Badgers	Seals	Hummingbirds
Pikas	Humpback Whales	Pumas	Lemonade	Llamas	Tulips	Ostriches
Sunflowers	Fennec Foxes	Sea Lions	Squirrels	Roses	Porcupines	Ice Cream

All covers credited: Victoria Blakemore
Series: Elementary Explorers

www.ingramcontent.com/pod-product-compliance
Lightning Source LLC
Chambersburg PA
CBHW051252020426
42333CB00025B/3168